Grandma's Tales and Travails

by Joyce Green

Grandma's Tales and Travails

Joyce Green

ISBN: 978-0-9969684-8-5

Library of Congress Control Number: 2025900965

Published and Printed in the United States of America

Joyce Green, *Grandma's Tales and Travails*

Illustrators: Eric Muchira, Torie Montrel, Michael Ayers Jr.

Publisher: G Publishing LLC

Editor: Anthony Ambrogio

This book is dedicated to my grandchildren and in particular to my granddaughter,

Sheyenne Nadeira Simpson

And to my grandsons,

Shaydon Isaiah Simpson and

Sequoyeth Ashton Simpson

Acknowledgements

I wish to gratefully give thanks to the following for their invaluable assistance in the creation of this book:

- Azikiwe J. Simpson: Consultant

- Gypsy Houston: Monroe, NC, Genealogy Librarian

- Julia Hunter: Publisher, G Publishing

Contents

"Oooh, You Telling a Story!"—"You Telling a Tale!"

Sometimes, my neighborhood friends and I would tell each other stories and exaggerate what happened. The more each one of us pretended that what happened in each of our stories was true, the more important we felt. This day, it was my turn.

Figure 1: Paula, me, and Gene.

We were sit-ting on my front steps. My friend Paula was next to me on my right. Gene, my close neigh-bor, was sit-ting on my left. I de-cided to tell them a tale about a *haint* (a ghost or goblin) lurk-ing at night in our back-yard.

1

I began. "It was a cold night. The wind was blowing real hard. I was looking at the full moon out my bedroom window. All of a sudden, I saw a spooky-looking gray shadow floating in the air. Then the gray shadow zoomed into our garage."

Figure 2: I saw a "haint."

"Oooh," Paula gasped and covered her mouth and nose with her hands. Gene frowned, tapping his feet nervously up and down.

Ma, who was in the house, was walking by the screen door when she heard us. She opened the door and came over to where we were sitting on the outside stoop.

As Ma stared at us, we looked at each other. I was filled with guilt. We were caught telling tall tales.

*****

Whenever we used our imagination to make a story bigger or different than what really happened, my mother (Ma) would say, "You're telling a tale!"— a tale being a story that, once we changed it, became mostly untrue: a falsehood or a fib.

A fib was supposed to be a little falsehood or even a fairytale. A fib was thought to be a little innocent untruth that wouldn't really hurt anybody. Some people outside of our community called a fib a little white lie.

But that wouldn't work for Ma, especially when me or my brothers and sister got caught telling her a fib. Ma would roll her eyes and look at us sternly and say, "You're telling a tale." We would close our mouths and try to ease out of the room in shame.

Forbidden Words!

I heard Registered Psychotherapist Julie A. Christiansen, in a February 2024 interview on the NPR radio station WABE 90.1 (Atlanta, Georgia), mention a chapter in her book, *The Rise of Rage*, called, "Maybe Swearing Will Help!"

Christiansen talked about a study she came across of two groups of people. In the study, one group was a control group. The other group was the study group. Both groups had to put their forearms in buckets full of ice. One group was allowed to swear (curse) as long as they wanted to while their forearms were in the ice bucket. The other group wasn't allowed to swear (curse) while their arms were in the ice bucket.

The purpose of the study was to see which group could withstand the cold pain the longest. The researchers discovered that the students who swore were able to keep their arms submerged in the ice bucket longer than the group who was forbidden to swear (curse).

The psychotherapist suggested that, if you have a wicked potty mouth, you will probably not get much effect from swearing when you get angry because your brain gets no added benefit. "It's just what you do."

But the psychotherapist implied that, when people who do not usually swear are affected by something that is extremely painful, whether emotional or physical, and let a curse fly, it mitigates the pain of that experience. Christianson stated, "Anger is what you feel, not what you do."

That interview took me back to old memories of an event that happened in the 1950s on Long Island in New York.

Joyce Green

*****

In those days, me and my brothers and sister were forbidden to say any curse words. Ma and Daddy NEVER used curse words, ever. So, it was an unspoken rule to never utter any curse words (or "cuss words," as we used to call them) at all.

A cuss word was a swear word. The Merriam-Webster dictionary defines a swear word as "**a term of abuse**; a derogatory term." I can attest to how abusive they are; I know that, when cuss words or swear words were directed towards me, they made me feel bad and small.

Words like "shut-up" or the word "lie" or "liar" were also bad words. In our house, especially if you were a young'un, those words were like "cuss" words too. Even the adults never said those words. What you *could* say was "You fibbing!" or "You telling a story!" That was a polite way of saying "You're lying" or "You liar!"

A lot of our neighbors had the same rules. They and their children never used cuss words. So, growing up, we weren't around "bad-speaking" people.

*****

When I was a little older. I started thinking about some things that happened in our house. I walked out our back door and sat on the back stoop. I began reminiscing. Ma's friend, Mrs. Mattie came to mind.

I recalled this one particular day when Mrs. Mattie, came over to our house in a frenzy. Mrs. Mattie had a new boyfriend named Mr. Frank. Before she acquired this new boyfriend, Mrs. Mattie had been widowed for three years.

It was a late Thursday afternoon. Mrs. Mattie's boyfriend, Mr. Frank, was at McCours' restaurant with a Thursday girl that he liked. Mrs. Mattie just happened to be coming through the building in the bus terminal, which was next to McCours' restaurant. Mr. Frank, was coming out the restaurant door with his arm around the other woman's shoulder. Mrs. Mattie saw Mr. Frank with the new woman.

"Uh-Oh!!!"

*****

At that time, many Black women who migrated to the north from the south found work as sleep-in maids or mother's helpers. These maids or helpers usually lived where they worked. They worked six days a week and got one day off—Thursday. On

Thursdays, the Colored (as Negroes were called then) maids or helpers got paid and came into town to have fun.

The words "Thursday Girls" were attached to the Colored maids and helpers. What people were unaware of was that the majority of the Thursday Girls were very naïve— young and innocent. They were ignorant about the behavior of the men they met and freely gave themselves and their money to the men they met.

The Colored Thursday Girls took pride in their appearance. Oftentimes, they wore shoulder-length wigs of slightly curled hair and tight, straight dresses (usually red) cut just above their knees. In those days, people thought that look usually meant the girls were fast (or loose) and a little shameful. But the Colored Thursday Girls hardly cared; they were dressed to the nines (looking fine).

Figure 3: A typical Thursday girl.

The Colored Thursday Girls who were maids and helpers usually took buses into town to the area bus station. When they got to the bus terminal, most of them were wearing high-heel shoes. They would strut down the bus steps, showing their shapely bodies and bosoms for all to see. And all did see.

The bus terminal would be teeming with people especially Colored men! Everyone knew that Thursday was the day that the Colored maids and helpers came to town with their pay in hand. They were looking for men and fun. On Thursdays, the men were there—clean as a whistle, decked out in their best outfits and two-tone shoes—ready to please.

*****

Well, when Mrs. Mattie saw Mr. Frank, her boyfriend, with the new woman, she exploded! She began screaming and cursing at her boyfriend and the new woman he was with. The new woman, the naïve Thursday Girl, was shocked because she didn't know that the man she was with had a girlfriend. The new woman, now furious and embarrassed, turned to Mrs. Mattie's boyfriend, and she too started cursing at him and calling him terrible names.

Everybody who was around the bus terminal and parking area came over to see what was going on.

Mrs. Mattie and the other woman ignored the little crowd that had gathered because they were too busy cursing and screaming at each other real loud.

Some lady said, "Look at those women; they don't have any home training! My goodness." An old-looking Black man yelled, "Ya'll don't have no respect for yourselves, hollering and screaming at that ugly man…you should be ashamed of yourselves."

The folks who were watching laughed at the yelling women and shook their heads in disgust. Then they started walking away.

Embarrassed and ashamed, Mrs. Mattie and the other woman settled down and quickly left the scene, leaving the boyfriend standing there. He watched them leave and turned around and went back into the restaurant.

After leaving the scene by the bus terminal, Mrs. Mattie came over to our house right away. She was very upset and began shouting and pacing back and forth. As she told Ma what happened, she began cursing while relating her story.

My brother and I were in the next room and heard them talking. We WERE SHOCKED!!! My eyes got big, and my mouth dropped open. I never heard anyone in our neighborhood use such cuss words …let alone a woman!!!

"Oooh!" my brother exclaimed. "—Did you hear that?" he whispered.

As she tried to calm Mrs. Mattie down, Ma must have realized that some of us children may have been nearby. Ma came into the next room where my brother and I were sitting. "Go outside!" Ma yelled at us. We did right away.

Later, after Mrs. Mattie had left, Ma called me into the house. My brother had gone across the street to play baseball in the field.

Ma said to me, "Sit down." I did.

Ma explained:

"Mrs. Mattie was really mad at her friend. She was so upset that she used a lot of curse words. It made her look very ugly. That's why we don't use curse words.

Figure 4: My mother, "Ma" (August 1962)

"When you curse, your face and body change. Your mouth and lips get real tight, and your tongue lashes out. Your eyes squinch up, and your forehead wrinkles up. Your body gets stiff and pokes out. Some people think that cuss words make them look fierce and strong. But it only makes them look ugly.

10

"Some people who don't like to be around cussing folks think they are better than those who cuss. They don't respect the cussers. And, if the cussers are girls or women, a lot of men start talking down to the cussing folks. The folks who don't cuss believe they are better than the cussing folks and that the cussers deserve to be treated bad. The folks who don't cuss believe that the cussers have no home training and that nobody taught them how to behave.

"You got home training, so you don't have to cuss or be loud in order to be heard or important. You're already important. RIGHT?"

"Yes, Ma, right" I said.

I often come in contact with folks (some young and some old) who are loud and use cuss words or other rude words to make their point and stand out. Most times, they are soooo attractive or beautiful-looking people who, in my mind, stand out as they are …

Even at my age today, I still remember Ma's words. and throughout my life, I have had very little need to use cuss words.

Back Home

My mother (Ma) was born on my grandparents' farm in Wingate, North Carolina, in July of 1914. When I was a girl, growing up, Ma's Momma and Poppa (my grandparents) still lived on the farm, which was deep in the country.

Every year in August, Ma and Daddy would take my sister, my brothers, and me and pack us up in the car so we could travel to our maternal grandparents' farm.

My three brothers and my sister were scrunched up in the back seat of the car with pillows and blankets wrapped around them. I was the youngest child and sat in the front passenger seat on Ma's lap.

We lived in Hempstead on Long Island. Daddy knew that the trip from Hempstead to Wingate, North Carolina, would take 13-15 hours. So we always traveled at night to avoid running into a lot of day-time traffic.

In the car, somebody was always farting, belching, or coughing. Sometimes we had to stop because one of us had to pee. When the boys had to pee, they would pee in a plastic jar that Ma put on the car floor next to the back seat. The boys would crouch over the jar and turn their backs to hide

their private area so nobody could see them ….
especially my older sister. "Whew," my sister said,
"that pee stinks."

When my sister or I had to pee, or do number two,
Daddy had to stop on the side of the road, to let Ma
get a roll of toilet paper out of the trunk. Then we
could wipe our butts. Most times, we girls would
pull down our panties and squat down near the
open car door and pee.

The boys (my brothers) always would heckle us
and yell, "Pee-*yew!* That stinks!" They were right;
it did stink. When we finished, we got back on the
road.

As usual, Ma had packed a food basket in the trunk
of the car. In the basket was fresh fried chicken, a
long loaf of white bread, and a pound cake baked
the day before. Most of the time, we had a gallon
jug of cherry or grape Kool-Aid. There were
napkins and plastic cups in a plastic bag next to the
food basket.

One time when we were traveling South (or "Down
Home" as Ma and her brothers and sisters called
it), we stopped at a Howard Johnson's restaurant
and motor lodge.

At one time, Howard Johnson's was a popular
chain of restaurants and motor lodges in towns and

on highways all across America. Howard Johnson's was known for ice cream and cheap food. The day we stopped there, my sister got me and her an egg-salad sandwich on white bread on a little white paper plate. I really wanted ice cream, but Daddy wouldn't have it. He thought it was wasteful. To Daddy, egg salad was a meal.

Once on the road again, Daddy continued driving south until we reached Highway 601 in North Carolina. "We are in the home stretch," I heard Ma say to Daddy softly. Daddy nodded.

Soon, Daddy turned off Highway 74 (the main road) to Walkup Road. My grandparents lived on Walkup Road in Wingate, North Carolina.

Walkup Road was a hilly, twisty two-lane road in the country. Most times when we got on that skinny road, it was during the night. There were no lights on that road, and it was pitch dark outside. All we could see was the moon shining through the branches of the trees or on the spooky cornfields. Thick shadows from the bushes, trees, and corn fields blanketed both sides of the road. It looked real eerie out there in the moonlight. That road terrified me.

Daddy drove down a steep hill, and soon the road got flat again. I saw the shadows of a big field of tall grass (which really was wheat) and big corn fields on both sides of the road. I shuddered as I eased down on Ma's lap below the window in the car.

Finally, we turned off that dark road into a big driveway next to a wooden house. The driveway was partly covered with gravel, and two other cars were parked there under a big tree. The air stank, and some animals were making noises in the distance. "We're here," Ma yelled from the front seat.

*****

I was always miserable when we visited grandma and grandpa. The air always smelled stinky; the animals, especially the dirty pigs, grunted a lot and looked nasty, and the cows were dumb.

All those cows did was eat grass and *mooooo* .... sometimes all day long. I never thought about milking any of those cows as I saw my cousins do. *Yuck*, I thought. Those cows were too ugly and smelly. They had long nipples hanging down under their stomach (I learned later that these were called "udders") and long skinny tails that would sometimes swat your head.

One thing that was sort of exciting, though, was that, whenever anyone arrived at my grandparents' house, no matter what time it was—even in the middle of the night—everyone, in the house got up out of bed to welcome you. Even the folks in those two parked cars under that big tree, where some of my male cousins were sleeping, woke up and got out the cars to welcome us.

Everybody made a big deal about every person and every child who just arrived. They made us feel special. I liked that.

For years, visiting my grandparents was a family tradition. After the passing of grandma and grandpa, one of my uncles took over the land and the farmhouse.

Changes!

In 1960, Daddy passed from an asthma attack. I was 13 then, and things had begun to change.

By the end of the 1950s and into the 1960s, Ma began working as a housekeeper and companion for one of the rich old White ladies in Garden City. Ma had learned how to drive and gotten her driver's license so she could take the old lady out, and the White lady's family brought a new 1955 white-and-gray Ford for Ma to drive the old lady around in.

Garden City was a town next to where we lived in Hempstead. Wealthy upper-class White people had lived. there for generations. They were said to be "wealthy" instead of rich because they had generational wealth, or old money. Their community was segregated on purpose. That's the way they wanted it to be, and it remained that way for years (even into the 2000s).

Several years later, the rich old White woman died. Her family stripped that car and other things from Ma immediately. They treated Ma like she was nothing and didn't matter. My brothers and I were very angry about the way she was treated. So we were amazed at how Ma just moved on afterward, as if the Whites' reprehensible behavior didn't matter.

Before she passed, that old White lady became quite fond of Ma. She taught Ma a lot about money and gave Ma a trip to Germany as a gift. She taught Ma about European social graces, such as dining etiquette, social behavior, and clothing styles. Ma taught us some of what she learned. It became very useful for us later in life. But Ma faced a lot of jealousy and envy from some of her sisters who didn't get exposed to those things.

Ma's Stories

Figure 5: Great Grandma Hannah.

Some Saturday mornings, Ma liked to sit on our porch and read the newspaper. She would cut out money-saving coupons for when she went shopping. Once in a while, while she was clipping coupons, I used to ask Ma about her childhood. She told me stories about great grandma Hannah Parker, the Influenza Pandemic, the Great Depression, cotton picking, and grandpa and grandma. Here are some of Ma's stories.

Great Grandma Hannah

Ma was born in 1914 in Wingate, North Carolina, she often recalled the stories that her momma (my grandma) told her.

"Your grandma Jessie (Momma) learned all about plants and herbs. Momma's mother (your Great grandma Hannah) would, on occasion, visit her children and teach them about natural medicine. When Great Grandma Hannah visited us, she would help with the chores."

"Great Grandma Hannah was very light-skin," Ma said, "and she had very long hair. Grandma Hannah always wore these long dresses. She would come to visit us and stay a month or two."

"Some days, in the late evening, Grandma Hannah would go deep in the woods across Walkup, which was a dirt road then, to pick healing plants and herbs."

Ma continued, "One evening, Grandma Hannah went across Walkup, the dirt road, deep into the woods across from our house. The sun was setting, and Grandma Hannah had waited until the evening when the plants and herbs were at their peak, full of good smells and medicine."

Ma said, "It was in the early 1900s, and Wingate/Marshville, North Carolina, was a little farming town. We used horses and buggies on the narrow, bumpy dirt roads, and walking long distances was normal.

"On this day," Ma stated, "Grandma Hannah was deep in the woods picking herbs and healing roots when she heard loud voices and the sound of horses. She saw a group of White men who were riding through the back woods. One of them saw her as she tried to hide from them.

"'Ooooh, lookie there, a darkie,' one of the men shouted. 'Let's get 'em!'"

They caught Great Grandma Hannah. It didn't matter that she was a woman. "'It looks like there's only one,' one on the men said. So the men whipped, tarred, and feathered Grandma Hannah, leaving her to die. Those men broke Great Grandma Hannah's jawbone and several ribs. Her long hair was gummy and matted with tar and feathers."

Ma said, "It got dark, and it was late. Momma was worried. Poppa and some other men started looking for Grandma Hannah. Once she was found by grandpa and others, they carried her back to the farmhouse."

Ma explained, "Great Grandma Hannah was never the same. She had to use a handkerchief tied around her head to keep her jawbone in place. She mumbled and dribbled a lot because of her injury. She walked hunched over with the aid of a stick and mumbled when she tried to talk.

"Grandma Hannah didn't live very long after that. She could barely eat food because of her broken jaw, but she still came to visit and show Momma how to do things when she could," Ma said.

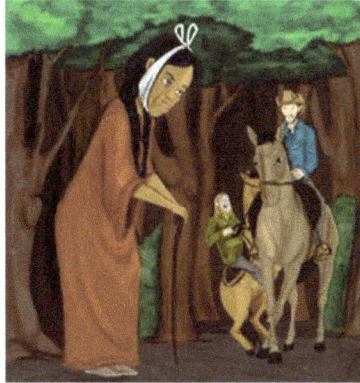

Figure 6: Great grandmother Hannah after the assault. Her White attackers pictured in the background.

The 1918 Influenza Pandemic

According to the 1910 US Census, the population in North Carolina was 2,206,287.

White	1,500,511
Negro	697,843
Indian	7,851

The population in 1910 in Union County North Carolina was 33,277.

In April 1919, Dr. William Rankin, the Secretary of the State Board of Health and a noted proponent of health education, reported the death of over 13,600 North Carolinians from influenza, and estimated that approximately 1 million of North Carolina's 2.5 million inhabitants had caught the disease. Nationally, the disease killed around 700,000, and some estimates suggest anywhere from 50 to 100 million died worldwide. (*Source: NC and Influenza (WWI); Public Health; Infectious Diseases*)

Ma told me that she was a little girl when the influenza pandemic hit North Carolina and in particular Union County where she lived.

I asked Ma what happened then.

Ma began: "It. was a cold, windy day on the farm, in 1918. I was about four years old. Momma and Poppa were talking real low about some sickness going around.

"Poppa was worried. He heard that many of his friends and some of their family members were sick or had died. Momma quietly told Poppa that she was going to give the young'uns some healing medicine and herbs to help fight off the sickness. Poppa nodded.

"Momma went to work boiling natural roots and herbs that she had gathered from the woods across the road from our house. Momma used turpentine and wild onions together. Momma had everybody take castor oil. She mixed some other stuff with some black molasses that Poppa had made.

"*WHEW,* that smelled and was bitter. We were all going to the outhouse (outdoor toilet) a lot. Then Momma rubbed cod-liver oil over our bodies and made us take some of that. She did that to Poppa and herself too.

Figure 7: Ma's parents, Sylvester and Jesse Cox in a formal studio portrait.

"The sickness was raging throughout the entire community. It was a long time before the sickness calmed down. Poppa kept people away from visiting us, and we did our chores as much as we could. Then the news got out. Many folks who lived sort of near us, had passed. Home-goings (funerals) were happening every day, sometimes twice a day. But Momma and Poppa never said a thing about them to us.

"We stayed in for days and told stories in the evenings around the pot-belly stove. For many days, we saw buckboard wagons taking away families who had died from the sickness. We were scared," Ma said. "Momma had Georgia, my little sister, and in 1919 was pregnant again with Ellen (Bright).

"Momma didn't lose one family member. After a while, maybe around 1920, people began coming out. They wanted to know what Momma and Poppa did to keep our family from getting the sickness. Poppa and Momma just smiled and nodded.

"Poppa continued to keep people away from us for a good while. We had to scrub the floors and walls in the house using brown soap, water from the well, and turpentine. We had to throw some mixture with water on the pigs and mules to keep them clean. We did that for a good while, and we never got sick. Months later, we found out about a lot of our neighbors who had died. We were sad but glad that Momma and Poppa knew how to take care of us."

The Great Depression

During the 1929 depression, North Carolina farmers faced enormous challenges from growing too much cotton and tobacco, which were the two main cash crops in the state. (From *Tar Heel Junior Historian*, published for the Tar Heel Junior Historian Association by the North Carolina Museum of History.)

From the crash of Wall Street in 1929 to America's entrance into World War II, about 25% of the North Carolina population was on relief programs. Nationally, 50 % of the population was out of work.

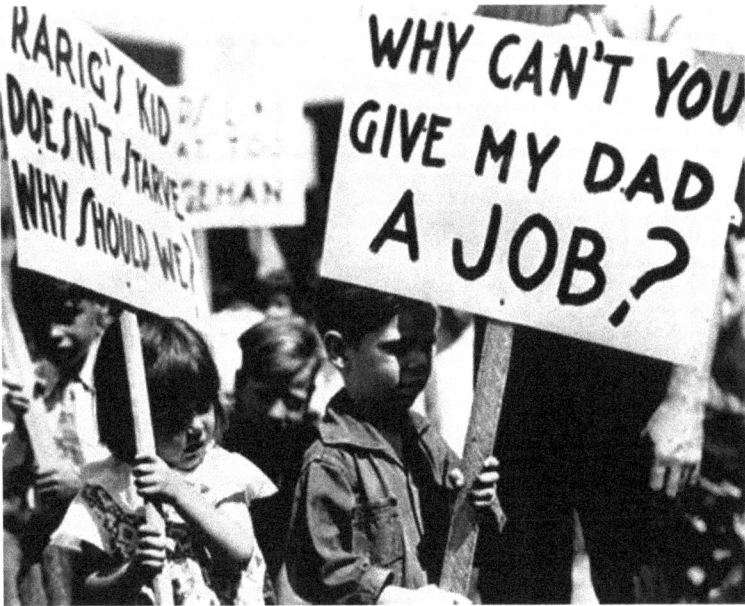

Figure 8: Inside the Story of The Great Depression | Education

During the Depression, vulnerable populations, like children, the elderly, and African Americans (due to the discrimination practiced against them) proved to be the hardest-hit groups.

Figure 9: Child victims of the Great Depression. Inside the Story of The Great Depression | Education

Many White folks felt entitled to the few jobs that were available. This left African Americans unable to find work. As a result of discrimination, the charges for farm machines and fertilizer, corporate purchases of small farmers' land, and political corruption and taxes caused many Blacks to lose their farms.

Some farmers, like my grandpa and grandma, were sort of fortunate. Before the Great Depression, Grandpa worked his children (especially the seven girls that were born before any boys) as rented laborers. They were share-croppers during the growing season and maids in the winter.

Ma often said, "Poppa grew cotton, tobacco, sugar cane, wheat, melons, and vegetables. We, my sisters and I, had to do all the plowing of the land, cotton picking, seed planting, and crop harvesting. When it was time to plow the land in the spring, we were pulled out of school to do it.

"When it was time to pick cotton or tobacco, we were pulled out of school. When cotton-picking or tobacco-picking time was over, we had to pick corn, tomatoes, and okra to be canned for the winter. Momma always put up (canned) sauerkraut, corn, tomatoes, and okra for the winter.

"Before harvest time was over, Poppa would rent us girls out to other farmers to plow and plant their fields. We worked all day long in other people's fields, plowing and plantin' seeds. Poppa always collected the money from our work.

"In between the times we were working for other people, we had to plow our own land to feed ourselves.

"At winter, Poppa rented us out as housemaids. We had to go clean the White folks' houses, do their ironing and washing. Back then, we used a wash board and that brown octagonal soap to wash the clothes clean.

"I used to get paid 50 cents a day for a full day's work. Poppa would be waiting for me to get home and then he took all of it. I hated that. I asked Poppa for 10 cents to buy some sweets once, and he exploded. He said, 'You ain't worth nothing, and you ain't gonna get nothing.' I cried for the rest of that evening.

"Many times, I would do extra chores for the Straws, the White family I worked for. Mr. Straws would give me a nickel and tell me, 'You hide and keep this for yourself. Don't tell anybody that you got this.'

"And I did just that. I hid my nickels under the house where the dogs slept.

"When the Depression hit, farmers who grew their own food and raised hogs, pigs, and chickens survived on vegetables, meat, and eggs. Their cows produced milk and cream for butter.

"Grandma and some lady neighbors had quilting parties while other women were making their family's clothes.

Figure 10: Quilting

"Times got real hard. People weren't selling cotton or tobacco as much. A lot of folks were hungry and suffering while trying to find food.

"Poppa saw hard times coming. He heard at our church (Piney Grove) that many church members were struggling to survive and hold on to their land.

"Momma had been puttin' up (canning) fruits and vegetables for the winter, as usual. Poppa was an excellent farmer. He would take tips from Grandma, according to the phases of the moon, and plant a lot of food crops.

Figure 11: Cousin Jack in Wingate learned from Grandma how to put up (can) fruit and vegetables like she did during the Depression.

"Poppa was a little famous. Ma told me that grandpa was in a newspaper or something, and my cousin Steve told me that it was the almanac. He was featured in a local almanac under a column called 'Vest Cox Says,' which offered tips about how he grew food.

"As time went by, food got harder to get. People were raiding houses and stealing folks' food. Poppa told Momma to put up a lot more food because we had a large family.

"At that time, Poppa had over 44 acres of farmland and a large number of acres across Walkup Road where the woods were. Poppa also had a number of acres of land on the main highway (Route 74), but, because he was a share-cropper, he couldn't pay for a wagonload of fertilizer. The White folks took that land from him.

"Poppa knew food raiders were on the march. So he went deep into the back of his land and dug a deep ditch. Poppa laid large flat boards across the bottom of that ditch. Then he nailed together wooden planks around all the sides of the ditch.

"Momma packed the extra canned vegetables and fruits in a buckboard. Poppa took the canned food to the ditch and packed them into the hole, laying wood planks on each row. When the ditch was nearly full, Poppa laid the last planks on top of the canned food and packed the left-over dirt back into the ditch. He took the remaining dirt to the field.

"As hunger continued to increase in the small town of Wingate, North Carolina, people got more vicious. One cold November evening, several months after Poppa had dug his storage ditch, we heard a loud noise of rumbling horses outside our house. Four White men came banging at our door.

"'Open up this da*@*#-! door!' they were shouting as they broke the door latch. They came in our house in a fury, going through the rooms, looking under the beds, and then into the kitchen. They were looking for food. They found some canned food under the bed and molasses in the kitchen. They stole what chickens they found and a pig. Then they left.

"Poppa was mad but not broken. He knew he had his storage ditch in the woods. That ditch saved our lives, and we made it through hard times without suffering."

Figure 12: Grandpa Sylvester and Grandma Jesse in their older age.

Ma said, "Because of how I was raised on the farm, it helped me and your Daddy hold on through the hard times here in New York. We worked hard even though we didn't have much *ed-u-ma-ca-tion.*

"Ha, ha, ha," she laughed. ("Ed-u-ma-ca-tion" is what Ma and her sisters used to call education when they were in school).

I smiled. I was proud of Ma and Daddy for putting up with all the things they went through.

Robert Franklin Williams

When I was visiting my grandparents in Wingate, North Carolina, I heard my mother, aunt, and uncle talk about a strong Black man who stood up against some angry White folks and the Ku Klux Klan. "That man stood his ground and fought to protect his and other Black farmers' land in Monroe, North Carolina," my Uncle Noel said.

Monroe is a town in North Carolina located across Highway 74. It is called the county seat of Union County.

Wingate, North Carolina, the little farming town where my grandparents' farm was and where my mother and her sisters and brothers were born, sits directly on the opposite side of Monroe off Highway 74.

Later in life, I often thought about the conversation Ma, her sister, and my uncle had about that strong Black man. I thought, *Who was this Black man?* It occurred to me that there might be some powerful stories about him in Monroe, North Carolina. Curiosity got the best of me. I decided to do some research.

I contacted the Monroe Public Library, which I had visited on several occasions many years ago. Little did I know that the person that I was going to research was one of the main activists who helped integrate that Monroe library.

After inquiring within the Wingate community, I found out that the strong Black man who stood up for local Black farmers and their rights was Robert F. Williams.

Figure 13: Photograph of Robert F. Williams, June 1971, (University of Michigan News and Information Services)

"Okay," I whispered under my breath, "this should be very interesting." Here's what I found out.

Encyclopedia Britannica: Robert Franklin Williams was born in the Winchester section of Monroe, North Carolina, February 26, 1925. Williams was a grandson of slaves and the son of a railroad worker.

In his late teens, Williams migrated to Detroit, Michigan. While in Detroit, he worked in an auto factory and was a member of the United Auto Workers union (UAW).

Robert Williams served 14 months in the Army after being drafted in WWII. He later enlisted in the Marines in 1954. He served in the US Marines from 1954 to 1955. He returned home to Monroe, North Carolina, in 1957.

Some researchers said that, after Robert Williams returned home, he became a civil-rights activist when he saw Monroe's police chief, Jesse Helms Sr., beating a Black woman. Shortly after that experience, Williams began fighting against racism.

In 1957, Williams was elected president of the local National Association for the Advancement of Colored People (NAACP) in Monroe.

I was familiar with the NAACP, but I really needed to know exactly what they stood for. So I looked them up.

The National Association for the Advancement of Colored People (NAACP) was an interracial American organization created to work for the abolition of segregation and discrimination in housing, education, employment, voting, and transportation. Its goal was to oppose racism and to ensure African Americans their constitutional rights. (*source*: NAAACP.org)

I continued with Williams' story. Williams gained notoriety internationally when various news agencies highlighted Monroe Whites' and the Ku

Klux Klan's refusal to allow Blacks to integrate Monroe's public swimming pool. The controversy and uproar over this issue continued later on when Williams intervened in the "Kissing Case."

Monroe's Public Swimming Pool

In 1957, Black folks tried to enter and utilize the public pool in Monroe, North Carolina. Local Whites and the Klu Klux Klan were enraged. Williams and the NAACP arrived on the scene. They put up picket lines around the pool. The NAACP demonstrated peacefully, opposing the pool segregation.

Some disgruntled Whites fired on the protestors. Although many police officers were present, they took no action, Williams and the NAACP were unsuccessful in integrating the pool.

In 1961, Williams once again attempted to integrate the local public pool in Monroe. Because Williams felt that there might be a possibility of attacks by angry Whites and the Klan, he had begun stockpiling guns. By now, he had embraced the concept of "meet violence with violence." The NAACP opposed the "meet violence with violence," stand and suspended Williams for embracing that concept.

36

After returning to the pool, Williams and his armed followers stood their ground against the local police and a White mob. Monroe Whites tried to appeal to Williams and other Black folks by making promises that Black folks would get their own separate pool sometime in the future. Williams and Monroe Black folks refused that promise. The town then filled the pool with concrete to avoid integration.

The Kissing Case

In 1958, Williams hired, a civil-rights attorney from New York City to defend two nine- and seven-year old Black boys who were accused of molestation. The boys were beaten, jailed, and sentenced to a reformatory for kissing a white girl on the cheek. The girl was their age. Their sentence was to last until they turned 21 years old. This became known as the Kissing Case.

Eleanor Roosevelt, the former first lady, called the North Carolina governor and was instrumental in getting the boys pardoned three months later.

October 28, 1958
Two Black Boys, Seven and Nine Years Old, Arrested and Jailed for Over Three Months After White Girl Kissed Them on Their Cheeks

Figure 14: The "Kissing" Case.

Wow, I thought, *I was only a year or two older than those boys then. How shocking!*

Williams embraced armed self-defense. Some folks thought that Williams helped to inspire the **Black Power movement, Student National Coordinating Committee (SNCC),** and the **Revolutionary Action Movement (RAM).**

I was still young then, with little understanding of the Black Power Movement, SNCC, and RAM. So I researched the organizations to get a better understanding.

Black Power

Black Power began as a revolutionary movement in the 1960s and 1970s. It emphasized racial pride,

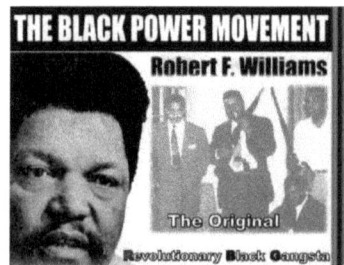

Figure 15: Black Power (National Archives)

38

economic empowerment, and the creation of political and cultural institutions. (*Source*: National Archives)

SNCC

SNCC was founded in early 1960 in Raleigh, North Carolina. SNCC's goal was to capitalize on the success of sit-ins in Southern college towns, where Black students refused to leave restaurants that denied them service based on their race. (*source*: https:// www.archives.gov › research › african-americans › black-power › sncc)

Revolutionary Action Movement (RAM)

RAM rallied for a "cultural revolution" that would purge the colonial White mentality from Black people in the United States. RAM's focus was to create a new, revolutionary culture by recapturing African aesthetics and art relevant to the revolution,

RAM wanted to move towards an active attempt to root out habits, traditions, customs, and philosophies taught to Black people by White oppressors.

RAM emphasized creating a black nation on land in Mississippi, Louisiana, Alabama, Georgia, Florida, Texas, Virginia, South Carolina, and

North Carolina. In their eyes, these lands rightfully belonged to black people.

When Robert F. Williams became chairman of RAM, he emphasized that all young Black revolutionaries must undergo personal and moral transformations.

Freedom Riders

In August,1961, the noted Freedom Riders rode through Monroe, North Carolina. Who were the Freedom Riders and what was their role?

Freedom Riders challenged racial segregation in American interstate transportation during the Civil Rights Movement. The activists traveled together in small interracial groups and sat wherever they chose on Greyhound and Trailway buses and on trains to establish equal access to terminal restaurants and waiting rooms. They brought racial segregation in the South to national attention. The riders demonstrated and challenged segregation law.

(*Source*: *Freedom Riders*, a 2010 American historical documentary film, produced by Firelight Media for PBS's *American Experience*. The film is based in part on the book *Freedom Riders: 1961 and the Struggle for Racial Justice* by historian Raymond Arsenault.)

Two weeks into the Freedom Riders' protest in Monroe, a mob of White supremacists attacked the Riders. As disgruntled Whites assembled, the Riders called for aid from the Black Guard. (Prior to the arrival of the Freedom Riders, Williams had applied to the National Rifle Association, or NRA, for a charter for a local rifle club. He called the Monroe Chapter of the NRA the Black Armed Guard.)

The Black Armed Guard

The Black Armed Guard was a national armed youth self-defense group run by RAM. RAM felt gang members could be trained to fight against White power structures instead of themselves.

The Black Armed Guard was made up of about 50-60 men, including some veterans. They were determined to defend the local Black community from racist attacks. (*Source*: Wikipedia, the free encyclopedia)

In Max Stanford's words, The Black Guard was formed "to stop our youth from fighting amongst themselves, teach them a knowledge of [Black] history ... and prepare them ... to protect our community from racist attacks."

At that time, Monroe had a large Ku Klux Klan chapter. The press estimated it had 7,500 members, while the city had a total of 12,000 residents.

During the confrontation, between the Freedom Riders and the Ku Klux Klan and local White mobsters in Monroe, a White married couple drove into the violence. Williams rescued the couple and let them stay at his house. White police misrepresented the rescue and charged Williams and others with kidnapping, even though there was no kidnapping report from the White couple.

There are several conflicting stories of what happened with "the kidnapping." The kidnapping version I tell is just one of the versions.

Williams, facing a kidnapping charge and possible violence and seeking safety from the Klan, collected his family and fled to Cuba.

While in Cuba, Williams wrote his book *Negroes With Guns*.

The book had a significant influence on the African American Defense League and the Black Panther party. Later, the book was developed into a documentary of the same name.

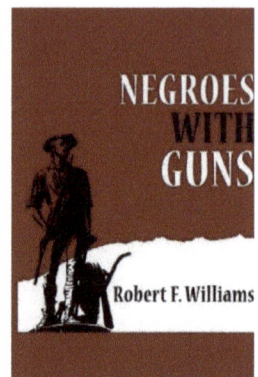

Figure 16: Book cover for Negroes With Guns.

While in exile, Williams traveled extensively internationally in Cuba, China, and throughout Africa. When living in Tanzania, Williams was named the first president of the Republic of New Africa.

In 1964, still in exile, Williams was elected president of the Revolutionary Action Movement (RAM).

After Williams returned to Michigan in 1969, he was arrested and extradited to North Carolina to face kidnapping charges. Williams was tried in 1975 and acquitted. In 1976, all charges against him were dropped.

Changes in his political position caused Williams to distance himself from the Black Power movement. He then began advising the State Department on its relations with China.

Williams lived the remainder of his life in Grand Rapids, Michigan. He died of Hodgkin's lymphoma in 1996 and was buried in Monroe, North Carolina, at Hillcrest Cemetery. (*Source*: Wikipedia). Rosa Parks spoke at his funeral.

In August 2023, Robert F. Williams became the first African American to receive a North Carolina Highway marker in Union County.

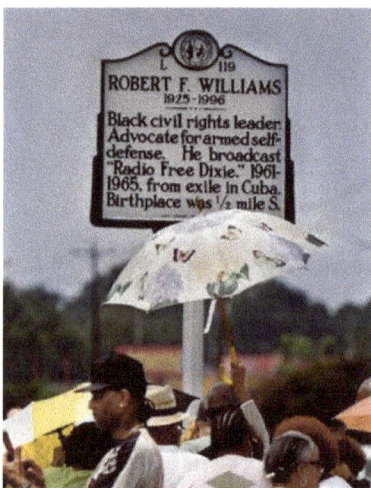

Figure 17: Robert F. Williams highway marker.

Wow! As indicated by his life's journey, Robert Franklin Williams was truly a hero for Black folks in Monroe, North Carolina. I am honored to research his journey and to share it with my family. Rest in Peace, Great One!

[This brief recapitulation of Robert F. Williams' history was reviewed for accuracy by Ms. Gypsy Houston of the Monroe Public Librarian of Union County, NC.]

Joyce Green

Cotton Pickin'

It was late August. The sun was hot that day, and a lot of flies were in the air. Big brown and green crawly bugs and things scooted across the dry barren ground in front of my feet. (*Ugh!* I thought as I quickly pulled my legs up close to my body.)

I was visiting my grandparents' farm. My mother, brother, aunts, uncles, and cousins, along with other family relatives who I didn't really know, were all visiting the farm in Wingate, North Carolina. It was our family-reunion time.

As I sat on the wooden boards of my grandparents' old porch, I watched Ma and her brother, my Uncle Noel, laughing and reminiscing about their childhood days on the farm.

Figure 18: Uncle Noel and Ma laughing and talking.

45

Suddenly, Uncle Noel leaned over and whispered something in Ma's ear.

Figure 19: Uncle Noel whispering in Ma's ear

They both howled with laughter. Then Uncle Noel started walking to his car and motioned to me to follow him. I scrunched my face and looked at Ma. She smiled and nodded her head approvingly. I walked to Uncle Noel's car, got in the front passenger seat, and looked out the open car window.

My nose was leaking. I wiped my runny nose with the back of my arm and shooed away the nasty flies and bugs. I listened to Uncle Noel hum a song as he started the car and backed out of the driveway next to the farmhouse. Uncle Noel drove down Walkup Road until he got to a little dirt road. He turned right on that road. There was a big bump at the head of the narrow, twisting two-lane dirt road.

46

On each side of the road there were long, deep ditches, which were like drains that caught run-off rain or melting ice or snow water.

About 10 minutes later, Uncle Noel pulled off to the side of that dirt road and parked under a large tree with long branches and big leaves. All I could see was huge cotton fields on both sides of the road.

Confused, I watched Uncle Noel reach over the front driver's seat, where he was sitting, to the back seat. He grabbed a big empty brown paper bag, and handed that bag to me. Uncle Noel said, "Go across the road there and fill this bag up with cotton."

"WHAT!?!" *I thought he was crazy!* I was 10 years old. I wasn't picking no cotton!! I looked at Uncle Noel with horror and disbelief.

Uncle Noel sighed and said, "Well, we gonna be parked here until you fill that bag up with cotton and feel what it was like to be a slave who had to pick cotton in the hot sun from dawn to dusk six days a week."

"Me, your momma, aunts, uncles, and some of your cousins had to pick cotton when we were little chill'in. Poppa and Momma and all of us was sharecroppers, so we ain't had no choice. We had to pick cotton to survive.

Figure 20: Two young Black girls pick cotton into their sacks |Source: Flickr.com

"So, little New York City gal, you're gonna feel what it's like to pick cotton today."

I was stunned.

Uncle Noel got out the car, opened the car back door behind the driver's seat, and grabbed some old yellow-looking newspapers off the floor. He slammed the back car door shut and spread some of those old newspapers on the hot car hood. Then he lay on top of the newspapers on the hood. He was going to take a nap. He said, "Wake me up when you fill the bag up with cotton."

Puzzled and angry, I just sat there.

After a half hour or so, I realized Uncle Noel was serious. The car seat was hot, and I was sweating while swatting a bunch of little flies. Uncle Noel was snoring.

Slowly, I got out the car and slammed the door. (I wanted to wake Uncle Noel up.)

I crossed the road and stepped over the high grass to the cotton field, constantly looking back at Uncle Noel, who was now awake, sitting up, and watching me. I wished I was bigger than him and not his niece. Maybe I would bop him and twist his arm to make him take me back to where Ma was at the farmhouse.

Figure 21: Me, forced to pick cotton and wishing I was big enough to bop Uncle Noel.

Looking at that BIG cotton field, I wondered if there were any snakes in there. Cotton was everywhere in that field. Where should I start? What should I do?

Uncle Noel yelled, "The cotton is in a round bulb. Each of dem bulbs has a seed in it. Some of dem bulbs has thorns on the branches. Pick the cotton piece out of the bulbs."

"What is a bulb?" I yelled.

Figure 22: Cotton ball.

"Ah...umm, gal, you don't know nothin' about cotton. The bulb is those round things on the plant. They look like a little brown cup with cotton pieces in it. Some of 'em has sharp thorns or stickers around it."

I gingerly stepped into the cotton field between two rows of cotton. I was sweating because I was so nervous. My hands were clammy, and I kept looking down at the ground. I wanted to make sure I wasn't stepping on any snakes or bugs.

I wanted to run out of that cotton field, but Uncle Noel told me I had to fill the bag with cotton before we would head back to the farm. *I hated him that day*.

I began pulling the bulbs off the cotton plant. "*Oh, no!*" yelled Uncle Noel, "you don't pick the whole bulb off the plant. Pull the cotton out of the bulb and put that into the bag, girl."

"That's not what you said before," I yelled back.

"Well, I'm sayin' it now," Uncle Noel shouted back.

I began picking the cotton, and the thorns pricked my fingers and hands. I rubbed my sticky fingers, trying to get rid of the little drops of blood from thorn pricks.

An hour later, after half filling the bag and wiping the dried, itchy tears from my face with the back of my hand, I ran out the field. I took the bag to Uncle Noel.

Uncle Noel slowly shook his head and gave me a drink from a bottle of water that had got hot in the sun. Exhausted, I listened as he reminded me that, as sharecroppers, he and Ma had to pick cotton when they were seven and eight years old. He said that, during slavery, his grandpa Otta (my great grandpa, who was a slave) and other slaves had to pick cotton from dawn (just before the sun rose) to dusk (just as the sun set), six days a week. They were punished and beaten if they stopped pickin'.

As Uncle Noel drove back to my grandparents' farm, I laid my head on the back of the car seat and closed my eyes. I thought about Ma and how hard that must have been. I thought about the slave children and how the thorns probably made their hands swell up and their fingers bleed like mine had.

When we got back to my grandparent's house, I opened the car door and ran over to where Ma was. I hugged her and cried for all of the slaves and the children who were sharecroppers. Uncle Noel looked at Ma, gave her the brown bag with the cotton that I had picked, and nodded. Ma looked at Uncle Noel and nodded back.

That night as I sat on the bumpy old bed in the dark bedroom off the eating room, I looked at my cousins, who were in bed next to me, snoring. Somebody's feet were sticking out of the covers, and they were smelly. Somehow, that didn't seem important now, as the four of us tried to find a spot on this one bed.

I looked out the window, which was about eight feet away. It was pitch black outside except for the twinkling stars in the night sky. My grandparents' farm was about 33 acres on this side of the road, so the farmland stretched as far as some trees you could see in the distance during the day.

I imagined all the work the slaves had done in the hot sun, day after day with no pay. I imagined all the children who had to work that hard just to live and stay alive. I thought about many of the little girls, younger than me, who had to pick cotton instead of going to school.

My eyes welled up with tears.

Figure 23: My eyes welled up with tears.

I wondered how many beatings Ma had gotten because she rebelled.

Then I thought, *Maybe the farm wasn't so bad after all;* it kept everyone alive.

Figure 24: Children picking cotton.

Figure 25: They're not easy to see in this photo, but this is Ma and her sisters picking cotton in Wingate, North Carolina in the mid-1920s.

Joyce Green

Watermelon & White Lightning!

My eyes popped open when I heard the sound of a crowing rooster. I was in a dark, spooky room lying on a bumpy bed, curled up (like a baby) in a fetal position. I carefully stretched my left leg out under the musty blanket. My toes touched somebody's cold, clammy leg. I jerked my leg back close to my body and held my breath as I pulled that musty blanket over my head. *Whose leg was that? Where am I? Where's Ma?* I thought nervously.

Frightened, I softly called, "Ma... Ma…" Then, when nobody answered, I screamed, "Ma, Ma, MAAAA!" and pulled that old musty blanket off my head.

"What's the matter with you?" a sleepy, low voice asked me. "Stop that noise!"

I recognized that voice. It belonged to my cousin Laney. Then I remembered where I was. I was in a bedroom at my grandparents' house in Wingate, North Carolina.

I sat up, wrapping that musty blanket around my shoulders. Then I heard some cackling chickens. *What an awful place*, I thought.

55

"Stop pulling the covers," yelled cousin Laney. Tears welled up in my eyes. Laney sighed.

There were two doorways in that dark room. One doorway led to the front room of the house, and the other doorway led off the kitchen. So now I knew where I was. But that didn't explain where Ma was!

Suddenly, a shadowy female figure appeared in the front-room doorway. "Ma?" I called out. But I knew it was somebody else because I could see that she had a pot belly and hair almost down to her stomach. It was that Grandma.

I trembled and began to cry, saying, "I want my mommy." She nodded and waved at me to get out of the bed and come out the doorway. Timidly, I did.

Then I heard Ma's voice outside. She was talking and laughing with her sisters. Ma had eight sisters, but only three of them were visiting at that time.

I bolted past Grandma and ran through the front door onto the porch, searching for Ma. I wanted to go back home to New York.

Ma saw me crying and running towards her. Ma stood up quickly and hurriedly started walking to meet me. "What's wrong?" she yelled.

"I wanna go home!" I screamed as I grabbed her skirt.

Ma put her arm around my shoulders and walked me over to where she was sitting with her sisters. She sat down in an old rickety wooden chair and told me to sit down, too. All I saw was an empty, dirty, rusty wood crate. Ma pulled that old crate next to her Then she motioned to me to sit on it. My face scrunched up at the sight of that crate, but I sat down. I sat down on the crate for what seemed like hours while Ma talked and talked with her sisters.

Ma's sisters (my aunts) began laughing and teasing Ma. They said, "You should've let your chillins stay here, on the farm, in the summer. Then they would be used to how we lived and grew up. That young'un has no idea of what it's like to be raised in the South on the farm. She doesn't know how hard it was and how strong it made us when we went up north to New York."

Ma snapped at them and said, "You old ones went to school and then went up north. But poppa pulled me out of school when I was in the third grade because he said I was strong and rebellious."

Ma continued: "Every time I turned around, momma was having babies. She always had a pot belly, so I thought that was just how she looked.

How was I to know that she was always pregnant? I had to take care of all those little babies, y'all, and even sister Lou's baby *and* momma until I was 13 years old. That's when I ran away up north, promising myself that, if I ever had any children, they would never, ever stay down south on this farm."

Ma was visibly annoyed. Her sisters were quiet because they knew Ma was telling the truth. When Ma got up, I followed her. I followed her wherever she went. I followed Ma around a lot that day.

Figure 26: Farming

Later that afternoon, two barefoot boy cousins came running to the front of the house. They were twins but not identical twins.

The twins had real dark, smooth skin. They wore blue-and-brown, sort-of dirty coveralls. They were skinny. Both the twins were about the same height but they looked different. One had a full head of hair while the other one looked like he was slightly balding on the top of his head. They laughed and affectionately pushed each other, telling each other little jokes. I thought they were real "country."

"Gwine out to the garden and get some melons," said the little ole grandmother to the twins as she continued rocking back and forth in a wooden, beat-up, noisy rocking chair on the porch.

"Yes Ma'am," yelled the twins.

Right next to grandma and grandpa's house was a big garden. The twin boys immediately took off running to the garden.

I was curious. So I tried to peek to see what they were doing. Ma saw me peeking and shouted to the twins, "Come get your cousin."

WHAT!!! I thought. My eyes got real big. What crossed my mind was, *I wasn't* that *curious.*

"Yes ma'am," said the twin with the most hair, and he started running toward me.

I panicked, but Ma said, "Go with your cousin to the garden. See what they're doing and what's growing there. Then help."

I looked at my cousin. He didn't have any shoes on his muddy, dirty black feet. *Ugh!* I thought. Reluctantly, I followed the big-hair cousin toward the garden. I looked back at Ma. She was busy talking to her sisters again. I walked on.

When we got to the garden where the other boy cousin was, I saw a bunch of melons.

One melon was freshly broken open, and the boy cousin who had been in the garden the whole time was munching on a piece of it that he had broken off.

"Yuck," I mumbled.

"What you say?" asked the slightly bald cousin who was munching on the melon.

"Nothing," I said.

"Yeah, you did," said the cousin who'd brought me to the garden.

"I did not," I shouted.

"You mumbled or somethin'," said the slightly bald cousin. I got quiet then, but they kept on talking. "You think ya somethin' special, but you ain't. If there was bad weather or a big snow blizzard, you wouldn't even know what to do. You don't even know how to grow your own food."

Figure 27: Cousins munching melon

"Yeah," said the big hair cousin, "you don't know nothin', city girl … trying to be all prim and proper-like and hanging on to your momma."

I wanted to leave that garden, but I got mad at them. I had to stand my ground. "I'm not acting prim and proper, but we just go to the supermarket and buy food. Not grow it." The twins looked at each other in amazement.

"You poor thing," whispered the slightly bald twin; "you don't know what real food taste like. *Uhhh-uhhh!*" He put his head down and shook it. I looked at them, wondering what they were talking about. Then the bald twin broke off a piece of the melon and offered it to me.

Oh no, I thought, *I better not refuse it.* I held my breath as I took a bite. *Mmm!* It was warm and sweet. I was surprised.

The sun was beaming down on our heads, and a bunch of little flying bugs were flying around near the melon. My hands were sticky and my mouth was dry. I told my cousins that I was hot, sweaty, and thirsty. I wanted to leave the garden. I needed to get some water and wash my hands.

"Where you goin'?" asked the slightly bald cousin.

"I'm hot and sticky," I said. "My throat is dry. I need some water."

The twins looked at each other. Then that slightly bald-headed twin said, "We got some water. We carry water all the time when we are out in the garden pickin' melons or vegetables. You can have some of our water." He reached in the back pocket of his overalls and pulled out a pint-sized bottle of clear liquid. He smiled and looked at his brother. The big-hair brother grinned.

"Take a big sip," said the slightly bald twin. "We had another bottle that we finished already. So drink up, gal!"

I took the pint and lifted it to my mouth. I took a real big swig to quench my thirst. "Oh, *oh*, OHH!" I screamed as I choked on the hot, fiery concoction. My eyes began watering; my nose started running; and I could barely breathe. I began to cough while holding my throat. I WAS ON FIRE!!! I fell to my knees, gasping.

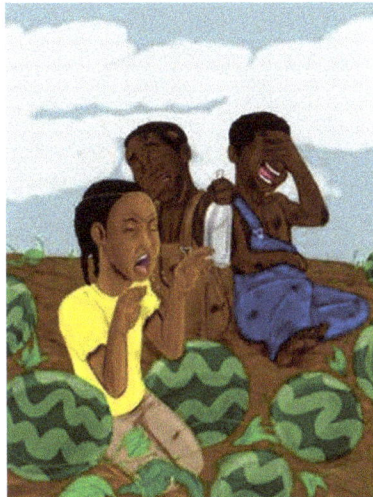

Figure 28: Me, suffering, while those two monster twins laughed their heads off.

Meanwhile, those two monster twins were holding their sides and rolling, on the ground, overwhelmed with laughter. I was furious but too miserable to speak. *WHAT WAS THAT STUFF?? IT SURE WASN'T WATER!!*

The twins laughed so hard that they could barely breathe. They sat on the ground next to the melon they were eating, trying to catch their breath. Their eyes were watering, and they used the back of their arms to wipe away the water.

I sat down on the ground too. I was aching all over. I wanted to attack them, but I was just too weak. "What *was* that?" I asked in a wispy, weak, shallow voice.

"Corn liquor," said the slightly baldheaded twin, grinning.

"Yeah," said the big-hair twin, "but some folks call it WHITE LIGHTNING or MOONSHINE!" He started laughing again, but this time, he tried to hold it because his sides and stomach hurt from laughing so hard earlier. I just sat there.

"Now you know something about the farm in Wingate, North Carolina," said the big-hair twin.

"Yeah, we christened you," said the slightly bald twin. I rolled my eyes at them. I was still too weak to yell at them.

Cautiously, I gathered some beans. The monsters grabbed several melons.

Joyce Green

We left the garden. Both of them were carrying big melons. I walked behind them slowly. It was a short walk to the house. The twins took the melons to the porch, and I walked to the side of the house where Ma was. She looked at me.

"What's the matter with you," she asked. There were dried tears on my face, and my nose was still running a little. "Were you crying?" she asked.

"No, the sun was just so hot when I looked at it that my eyes started running," I said.

By now the twins came walking around the side of at the house, looking like angels. "How did it go?" asked Ma.

"Little 'cuz did good," said the slightly bald-headed twin.

"Yeah," agreed the big-hair twin, "she learned a lot in the garden." They both grinned.

I looked at those twins and thought, *You just wait until I feel better; I'm going to get you back.*

I went over to the water pump to drink some real water and to splash some on my face.

Figure 29: Water pump

The twins came running over to the water pump and started pumping water for me. No one said a word.

Years Later

Little did I know that Moonshine—often called White Lightning—was a term used to refer to high-proof distilled spirits that were produced illegally. Moonshine was almost as valuable as real money.

Back in the days of prohibition, people made Moonshine at night because making and selling it was illegal.

Prohibition is the shorthand name for the prevention by law of the manufacture and sale of alcohol. Prohibition with a capital P refers to the period in the US from 1920 (when the 18th amendment to the Constitution made prohibition the law of the entire country) until 1933 (when the 21st amendment repealed it).

North Carolina was the first state in the nation to approve prohibition. On May 26, 1908, North Carolina approved the prohibition of the sale of alcohol in the state. North Carolina passed prohibition 12 years before the law was passed for the entire US.

The reason for Prohibition was to control people's negative behavior, presumed to be caused by alcohol consumption, which was thought to promote domestic violence and child abandonment. But, of course, many law-abiding adults liked to take a drink now and then—and, when drinking was prohibited, it became a kind of "forbidden fruit" that lots of people just *had* to try.

The unfortunate effect of Prohibition was to turn these law-abiding folks into law-breakers and to make the way for organized crime (run by people like Al Capone) to create vast criminal empires.

In places like North Carolina, independent bootleggers (people who made or sold alcoholic liquor illegally) got an early start on bootleggers and rum runners who began operating after Prohibition began. These people would use souped-up cars (as runners) to deliver the moonshine to other folks or to speakeasies—illegal drinking establishments which sold the liquor to their customers.

Since they made and sold the liquor undercover at night, that's how it acquired the name of "Moonshine." ("White Lightning" is a different matter; you can understand from what that clear, or "white," liquid did to me why it might be called "lightning.")

Some White men felt that the value of Moonshine was almost equal to gold and would use it as barter (exchanging it for other goods or services in place of money).

Even some Black folks took chances to make Moonshine whiskey to be sold. For a little history about that, see "African American Moonshiners and Bootleggers," YouTube·greenmentch,·May 26, 2021.

And, even after the end of Prohibition, people in places like North Carolina continued to operate their own stills and make their own Moonshine. Just ask my two cousins in the 1950s.

The Juke Joint

Before and after the era of slavery, Black folks didn't have many places to hang out and party. So they would use little places on or near the plantation as a refuge (a safe area, one shelterd from danger or difficulty). These places became known as juke joints.

"Juke joint" was the name given to a place where people could gather to drink, gamble, and dance, where local musicians played all types of music, although—at most of the juke joints—the Blues was the most popular music.

According to Wikipedia, the word *juke* comes from the language of the Southern United States Creole folks known as Gullah, in which *juke* or *joog* means "wicked" or "disorderly." Wikipedia further adds that, during Prohibition, juke joints in the South were rarely called juke joints but went by names like "Lone Star" or "Colored Café" and were usually only open on weekends.

Because of Jim Crow laws that kept Blacks out of most establishments, juke joints became their refuge and helped to relieve the stresses of hard physical work and the segregated containment of many Black folks.

By the Jim Crow era, Black-owned juke joints offered music and good food throughout many Black communities.

*****

One late-August day in the mid-1950s, my cousins and I were sitting in a few raggedy wooden chairs under the big tree in my grandparents' yard in Wingate, North Carolina. The tree's long branches and leaves towered over a wide dirt-and-gravel area where family members could park their cars near the farmhouse. It was family-reunion time, and most of us were visiting from the North.

We were grumpy, sweaty, and totally bored.

All of a sudden, Aunt Jozel (my youngest aunt) came running out the farmhouse door. "Ya'll get dressed and come on. Let's take a ride," she shouted to me and a couple of my cousins.

Jumping at the chance to get away from the farm, we quickly ran inside to change our clothes. I threw on a green-and-blue dress (one of my favorite dresses), which was slightly wrinkled.

When my cousins and I got back outside, we noticed Aunt Jozel's sisters (my aunts) and my uncles looking at her curiously. They knew she was adventurous and wondered what she might be up to, but they didn't question her because she had us young'uns with her.

Aunt Jozel chuckled under breath as we all got into the car. And off we went!

None of us young'uns had any idea where we were going, but Aunt Jozel knew.

Besides, we didn't care; we were leaving the farm.

Off we went! It seemed like we were riding for a *looonngg* time. But Aunt Jozel just kept looking out the window and hummed on occasion.

After a while, we got off the main road and turned onto a narrow dirt road. We were in the woods. Though it was early evening, it looked spooky. "Aunt Jo, where we going?" somebody asked.

"You'll see," said Aunt Jozel; "we're almost there."

About 30 minutes later, we pulled into a big open space where a lot of cars were parked. My cousins and I looked at each other. There was a big shabby-looking wooden house right in the middle of that big space. We smelled food; somebody was cooking what smelled like fried fish. And we heard music.

We were at the JUKE JOINT!!

"Okay, y'all can get out now," Aunt Jozel said. We slowly eased out of the car.

"HEY, SWEET THANG, c'mere and give me some sweetness," a dark-brown-skinned whiskey-smelling baldheaded man called out. He was leaning against a shabby wooden door in front of the colored juke joint.

"Who you talkin' to?" Aunt Jozel yelled back indignantly as she stepped out of the beat-up 1949 black Chevy.

"You …. sweetness," the man shouted.

"Man, you better go on outta here! Don't you see my nieces and nephew here with me?" she asked.

"Oh, I didn't mean no harm," he said softly.

"Uh huh," she said, eyeing him cautiously.

My Aunt Jozel was my Uncle Noel's twin sister and the youngest of my mother's eight sisters. Aunt Jozel was more of a rebel in her younger days, more so than her older sisters. She loved parties, dancing, and going to juke joints. We found out later that the owner of this juke joint was Aunt Jozel's boyfriend.

We looked around. A lot of Black folks were going into the wooden building. Each time the door opened, we smelled fish frying and heard loud music. We got hungry. All that activity made things sort of exciting but a little scary too.

Aunt Jozel knew everybody. When folks saw her, they would yell out her name and say "Hello!" I wondered how Aunt Jozel knew so many people.

My brother told me many years later that the owner of the juke joint (Mr. Horace) and my aunt owned the place together. *Oh*, I thought, *that's why Aunt Jozel brought us to the juke joint.*

Back at the juke joint, my aunt gathered us together. "Stay here together," she told us. "I'll be back in a few minutes."

Confused, we huddled together next to the car. Curious, we watched folks pull up in their old cars and trucks. They smoothed their clothes and patted their hair as they prepared to go inside the juke joint. They were funny.

About 15 minutes later, Aunt Jozel returned to the car where we were waiting. She was carrying four fried-fish sandwiches on white bread. Our faces lit up. As she gave us the hot sandwiches, we beamed with excitement and gratitude. We all were real hungry.

By the time we had finished half of our sandwiches, things changed.

A large crowd of Black folks was in the parking area of the juke joint, getting ready to go inside.

Suddenly, a car with some flashing lights pulled into the parking area and pulled up near the door.

Everybody who was outside stopped talking. The car door opened, and a huge-bellied White trooper got out of the car.

"What you niggras doing 'round here?" he asked.

There was total silence with in the crowd. The only thing you could hear was the music that was playing inside the juke joint.

Though he was alone, that trooper knew he was more powerful than all those Black people put together.

I looked around, and no one said a word.

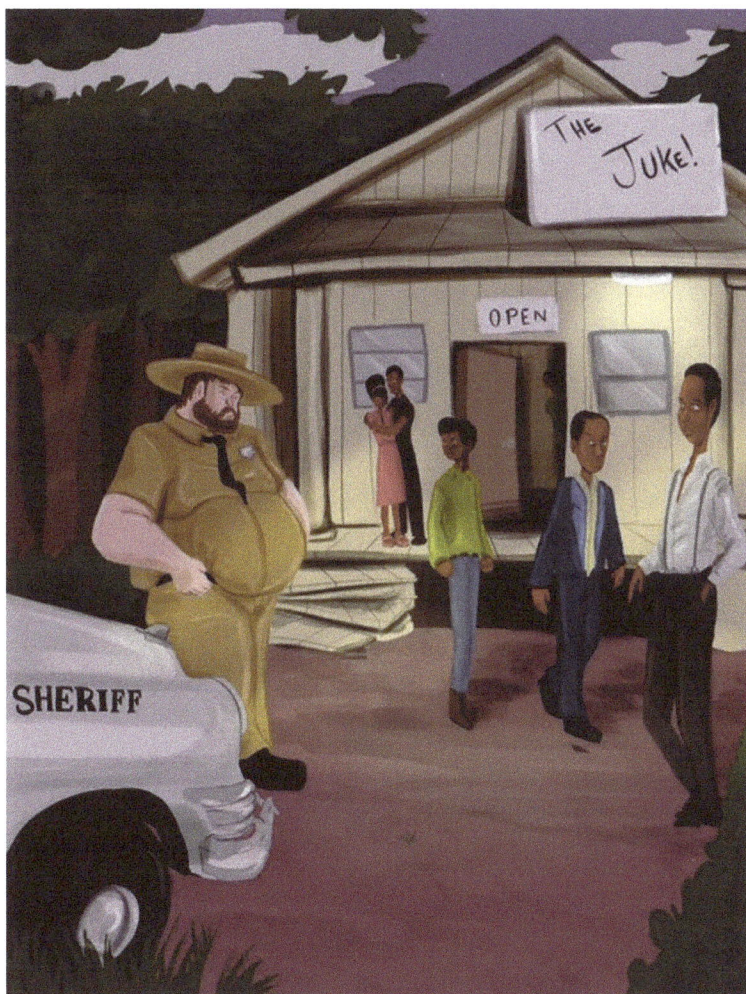

Figure 30: "What you niggras doing 'round here?"

Then the door opened. Aunt Jozel's boyfriend came out of the juke joint and said something low to the trooper. The trooper nodded, and then the two of them went around the side of the building to the back.

Fifteen minutes or so later, the smiling trooper and the grinning owner came from the back of the building. The owner and the trooper seemed mighty friendly when they came from the back of the juke joint.

The owner asked the trooper, "You want a fish sandwich?"

"I believe I do," said the trooper as he patted his bulging right pocket.

The owner quickly went inside, got the sandwich for the trooper and came back out to give it to him. The trooper patted his pocket again, took the sandwich and went to his car.

Some of the folks who were waiting to go inside were whispering to each other that the trooper was paid off so that the juke joint could keep its business going.

Ten minutes later, he pulled out the parking area, turned off his lights and was on his way. With a sigh of relief, the owner said to the folks outside, "Y'all come on in." A few folks left, but most out of them went inside.

We kids never went inside, but the door was left open, so we could hear the good music and watch some of the folks dance. They looked good dancing, and the music sounded nice.

I told my older cousin the story about our experience at the juke joint with Aunt Jozel. He laughed and said, "I was there!"

WOW!! I thought.

Figure 31: A typical juke-joint exterior--an unassuming façade disguising the joy, music, and good food within.

*****

Other Black people tried to open Juke joints, usually with little success. But, according to his granddaughter, Katherine Debrow, Horace Chambers Rutherford (1896-1960) built a juke joint open to all people prior to integration.

In an interview Sally and Gary Biggers conducted in 2006, Katherine Debrow described her grandfather Horace Rutherford, and Roseland Gardens. According to Debrow, Roseland Gardens served as a venue for music, church picnics, and, at times, the sale of "corn liquor." Debrow recalled that Sheriff Laurence Brown and Horace Rutherford were "very good friends." (So maybe he didn't need to pay the sheriff a bribe the way my Aunt Jozel's co-owner did with his state trooper.)

Horace Chambers Rutherford built Roseland Gardens around 1920, possibly as early as 1918, when he saw a need for a social gathering place for his friends and neighbors during a time when segregation prohibited the Black community from patronizing area restaurants, bars, pools, lakes, and music venues.

"People were coming here from all over—from Ridgecrest and Blue. Those people had no way of socializing other than church," said Debrow. "That's why my grandfather built the juke joint."

Figure 32: Dancers at Roseland Gardens, c. 1950. Photo courtesy of the Swannanoa Valley Museum & History Center

Roseland Gardens' 'reputation for lively entertainment spread quickly. Soon folks from as far away as Asheville, Old Fort, and Marion regularly made their way up the narrow dirt road to Black Mountain's Brookside community. Live music, performed by traveling musicians on juke-joint circuits, helped keep patrons on their feet and dancing.

Said Debrow, "Everybody always says to me, 'Your grandfather had the best music in town.'"

Figure 33: High-steppin' at the Roseland.

In 1950, a short article in *The Asheville Citizen*, as it was known then, identified Roseland Gardens as "the largest private recreation center for colored people in Western North Carolina." The center was open for the summer, held twice-weekly dances and movies, and provided "facilities for picnics, croquet, horse-shoe pitching, barbecues, and other forms of entertainment."

"It was also a theater once a week," Debrow said. "On Fridays and Saturdays, the kids could go to the theater…the front of the building appeared like an actual theater. You could walk up to there and buy your ticket…. for 10 or 15 cents.

"We watched Roy Rogers, Red Rider, the Phantom, and all of those old classics. My grandfather did that, thinking of the children in the Valley not having any entertainment.

"There was no other Black theatre in this area."

Roseland Gardens closed in 1976. Its buildings stood until the early 2010s.

Figure 34: Newspaper ad for the 1943 serial The Phantom, © *Columbia Pictures.*

Jim Crow

Figure 35: Union County Public Library, Monroe, North Carolina, where the author did much of her research, aided by librarian Gypsy Culp Houston.

King Cotton

By the 1850s, the cotton grown, shipped, and sold by Southerners was worth more than all the rest of America's exports put together.

The success of the industry was due to the Black slave labor that picked and sorted the product.

For around a hundred years after the Emancipation Proclamation Act of 1863, many freed Blacks remained cotton workers.

Joyce Green

Confederate States

Three months after Abraham Lincoln's election on November 6, 1860, the Confederacy emerged.

"On February 4, 1861, representatives from South Carolina, Mississippi, Florida, Alabama, Georgia and Louisiana met in Montgomery, Alabama (with representatives from Texas arriving later) to form the Confederate States of America." (From Confederate States of America Facts | Britannica)

Shortly after, four states from the upper South (Virginia, Arkansas, Tennessee, and North Carolina) also joined the Confederate States. (Britannica)

These states seceded from the union, and, in April 1861, Confederate forces fired upon Fort Sumpter, initiating the War Between the States, the Civil War, which culminated in the preservation of the union and, eventually, the dissolution of slavery.

Emancipation

On April 16, 1862, President Abraham Lincoln signed into law the "Act for the Release of Certain Persons held to Service or Labor within the District of Columbia." This act gave former slave owners, as a reparation payment, $300 per each enslaved person set free. (See "There Was a Time Reparations Were Actually Paid Out—Just Not to Formerly Enslaved People" in the online UConn Today website.)

Then the Emancipation Proclamation Act of 1863, signed by President Abraham Lincoln, declared "that all persons held as slaves" within the rebellious states "are, and henceforward shall be free."

Nonetheless, formerly enslaved African-Americans got nothing for generations of stolen bodies, snatched children, and labor other than their release from legal bondage. ("When Slaveowners Got Reparations," Tera W. Hunter, *The New York Times*, April 17, 2019)

Embracing Share Cropping to Survive

After slavery ended, freed slaves and their families were released with absolutely nothing. They had no food, clothes, housing, or land. Their survival depended on them becoming share croppers.

Like many other Black folks, and even some White folks, my great grandparents, my grandparents, and their children became share croppers.

Share cropping and poverty forced many Black families to be tied to the land to work just to survive. (Wikipedia)

Share cropper: A share cropper is a person who enters into an agreement with a land owner to farm the land and then pay a portion (share) of the produce as rent. (The American Heritage Dictionary of the English Language, 5th Edition)

Share cropping was hard work, which provided few benefits after a long day of plowing fields behind mules, planting seeds, and picking cotton, fruits, and vegetables during harvest time,

Reconstruction

Several years after the Emancipation Act was passed, Reconstruction came into being.

Reconstruction (1865-1877) was the effort to reintegrate the Southern states of the Confederacy and four million newly freed people into the United States after the Civil War. (history.com https://www.history.com › Topics › Civil War)

It was during Reconstruction that the 13th and 14th amendments (abolishing slavery, guaranteeing citizenship, and giving Black males the right to vote) were ratified. (Southern states were required to ratify these amendments before they could be readmitted to the union.)

The conventional end of Reconstruction was 1877, when the federal government withdrew the last troops stationed in the South as part of the Compromise of 1877. (Reconstruction era - Wikipedia)

Freed Blacks worked to reestablish their humanity during the Reconstruction period and after; however, once Reconstruction ended, Southern White-dominated state legislatures' goals were to disenfranchise and remove any political and economic gains made by African Americans during the Reconstruction era. (Wikipedia, the free encyclopedia)

From that time on, these Southern states enacted racial-segregation laws. These laws became popularly known as Jim Crow laws. They remained in force for almost 90 years, from the end of Reconstruction in 1877 until 1965. (See "American History: The Civil War and Reconstruction: Aftermath of the Civil War," LibGuides at John Jay College of Criminal Justice, CUNY, https://guides.lib. jjay.cuny.edu › c.php)

Jim Crow Laws

The Jim Crow laws were state and local laws that enforced racial segregation in the southern United States and in other areas in the late 19th and early 20th centuries. (Wikipedia, the free encyclopedia)

Jim Crow laws mandated racial segregation in all public facilities in the former Confederate States of America and in other states (Wikipedia, the free encyclopedia)

Where Did Jim Crow Come From?

Jim Crow came from the North. Thomas Dartmouth Rice, a White man who was born in New York City in 1808, began performing an act he claimed was inspired by an enslaved Black person. In the 1830s, Rice painted his face black and did a song and dance which was supposed to imitate Black people. The act was called "Jump, Jim Crow" (or "Jumping Jim Crow").

"He would put on blackface makeup, put on shabby dress that imitated in his mind—and white people's minds of the time—the dress and aspect and demeanor of the southern enslaved black person," says Eric Lott, Professor of English and American Studies at the City University of New York Graduate Center, in his book *Love and Theft:*

Blackface Minstrelsy and the American Working Class.

The Jim Crow show was a minstrel show which exploited stereotyped speech, movement, and physical features attributed to Black people in order to mock them.

Rice's act helped popularize Jim Crow as a derogatory term for African Americans. "It entertained, and miseducated, whites at the expense of Blacks for Rice's financial benefit,". Lott says.

Experts don't really know how a racist performance in the North came to represent racist laws and policies in the South, says the Director of the Jim Crow Museum and Vice President for Diversity and Inclusion at Ferris State University in Big Rapids, Michigan.

The Effect of Jim Crow

Jim Crow institutionalized economic, educational, political, and social disadvantages and second-class citizenship for most African Americans living in the United States. (Wikipedia, the free encyclopedia)

The Jim Crow laws mandated racial segregation in all public facilities in the former Confederate States of America, and Jim Crow became the term to describe a system of racial apartheid in the American South, with lingering effects today.

Jim Crow dictated racial segregation most infamously through racial segregation in schools and public spaces.

(Source: https://onthebooks.lib.unc.eu/laws/the-laws-in-context.)

The Black Codes

The Southern states implemented the Black Codes to augment Jim Crow laws. Black Codes severely restricted the rights of Black people, who were now supposed to be free. These codes limited what jobs African Americans could hold, and their ability to leave a job once hired. Under the Black Codes, some states also restricted the kind of property Black people could own. (National Geographic Society, Encyclopedic entry, "Black Codes and Jim Crow Law")

Beginning in the 1870s, Jim Crow laws were upheld. in 1896 in the case of Plessy v. Ferguson, in which the Supreme Court laid out its "separate but equal" legal doctrine regarding facilities for African Americans.

However, facilities for African Americans were consistently inferior and underfunded as compared to facilities for Whites.

Jim Crow institutionalized economic, educational, political, and social disadvantages while promoting second-class citizenship for most African Americans in the United States.

Many White Christian ministers and theologians taught that White people were the Chosen people, Black people were cursed to be servants, and God supported racial segregation.

Newspaper and magazine writers routinely referred to black people as niggers, coons, and darkies; their articles reinforced anti-Black stereotypes. Even children's games portrayed Black people as inferior beings.

The Jim Crow system (as indicated in the Jim Crow Museum) had the following beliefs or rationalizations:

- White people were superior to Black people in every way, including intelligence, morality, and civilized behavior;

- sexual relations between Black people and White people would produce a mongrel race and would destroy America;
- treating Black people as equals encouraged interracial sexual unions;
- any activity promoting social equality encouraged interracial sexual relations;
- when necessary, violence must be used to keep Black people at the bottom of the racial hierarchy.

Jim Crow also had its system of etiquette.

Jim Crow Etiquette

A Black male could not offer his hand (to shake hands) with a White male because it implied being socially equal.

A Black male could not offer his hand or any other part of his body to a White woman, because he risked being accused of rape.

Black and White people were not supposed to eat together. If they did eat together, White people were to be served first, and some sort of partition was to be placed between them.

Under no circumstance was a Black male to offer to light the cigarette of a White female—that gesture implied intimacy.

Jim Crow etiquette prescribed that Black people were introduced to White people, never White people to Black people. For example: "Mr. Peters (the White person), this is Charlie (the Black person), that I spoke to you about."

White people did not use courtesy titles of respect when referring to Black people, for example, Mr., Mrs., Miss., Sir, or Ma'am. Instead, Black people were called by their first names.

Black people had to use courtesy titles when referring to White people, and were not allowed to call them by their first names.

Black people were not allowed to show public affection toward one another in public, especially kissing, because it offended White people. (Wikipedia)

If a Black person rode in a car driven by a White person, the Black person sat in the back seat, or the back of a truck.

White motorists had the right-of-way at all intersections.

Stetson Kennedy, the author of *Jim Crow Guide* (1990), offered these simple rules that Black people were supposed to observe in conversing with White people:

- Never assert or even intimate that a White person is lying.
- Never impute dishonorable intentions to a White person.
- Never suggest that a White person is from an inferior class.
- Never lay claim to, or overly demonstrate, superior knowledge or intelligence.
- Never curse a White person.
- Never laugh derisively at a White person.
- Never comment upon the appearance of a White female.

You can find these rules and more listed at the Jim Crow Museum.

North Carolina

Figure 36: Sign for bus segregation in North Carolina.

Segregation was present in all aspects of life, even in the library systems in North Carolina.

Rules in the Libraries:

An 1889 law stated, "Books shall not be interchangeable between the White and colored schools, but shall continue to be used by the race first using them." (Hornsby, Alton Jr. (23 August 2011. *Black America: A State-by-State Historical Encyclopedia* [2 volumes] ABC-CLIO. ISBN 9781573569767. Retrieved 30 August 2017 – via Google Books.)

"The state librarian is directed to fit up and maintain a separate place for the use of the colored people who may come to the library for the

purpose of reading books or periodicals."
(Wikimedia Foundation, Inc.)

How Jim Crow Affected Me and My Family Personally!

Some effects of the Jim Crow era had a deep personal impact on my family. A year after my mother was born in July of 1914, in Wingate, NC (which was approximately three miles from Monroe, NC), there was a land sale.

The big lots (located four miles from Monroe, N.C.) were property made available for land sales to Whites only. No sales to Colored People.

The land was a short distance from my grandparents' home. They were sharecroppers then. However, they were forbidden from purchasing or having any access to the available land in the area.

Figure 37: Monroe, NC. Big Lot and Land Sale contributed and highlighted by Gypsy Culp Houston, Genealogy & Local History Librarian, Union County Library, Monroe, North Carolina.

Whites were happy to engage in segregation and to be able to possess low-cost land in the Monroe, NC, area.

Years later, the influence of Jim Crow continued to flood the counties of North Carolina. For example, in 1948, flyers and advertisements were spread among various communities, celebrating the coming minstrel shows which mocked and denigrated African Americans.

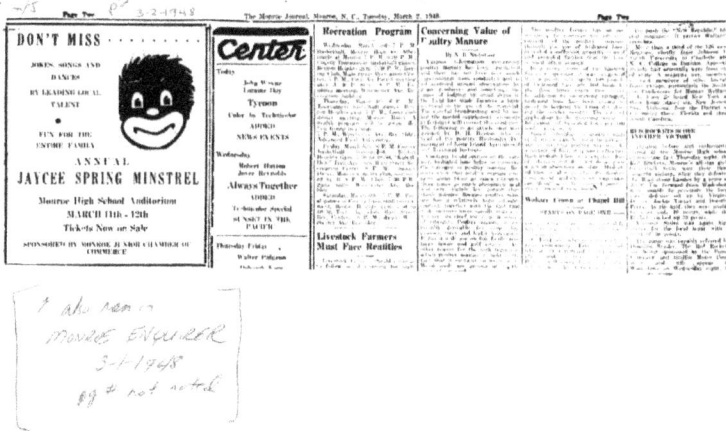

Figure 38: Monroe, NC. Minstrel Show highlighted by Gypsy Culp Houston, Genealogy & Local History Librarian, Union County Library, Monroe, North Carolina.

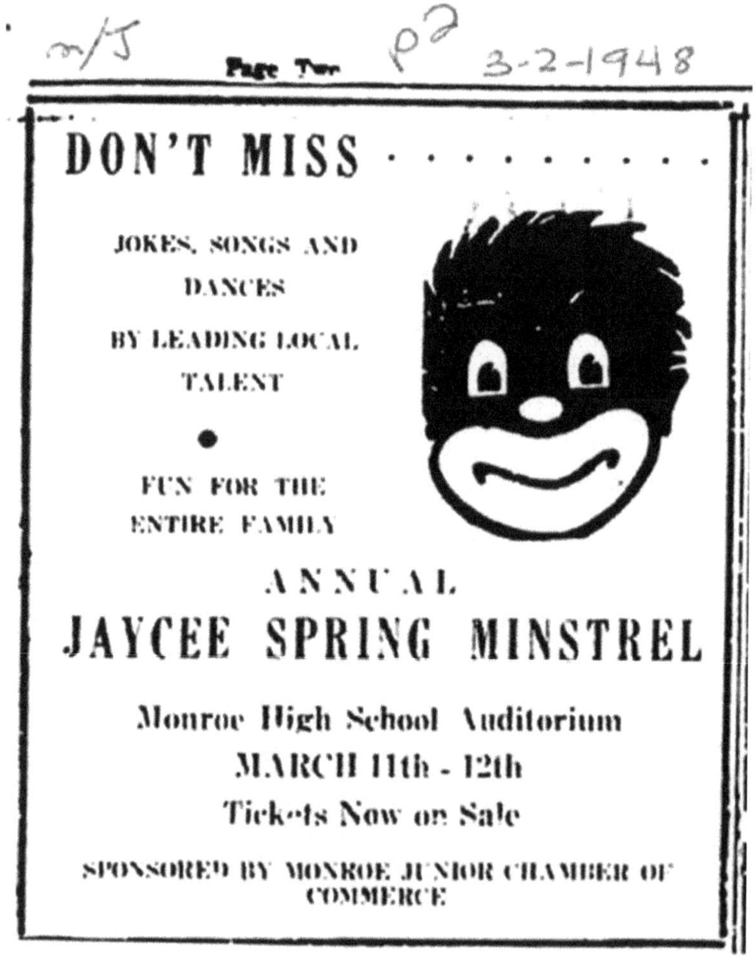

n/J   Page Ten   p2 3-2-1948

DON'T MISS · · · · · · · ·

JOKES, SONGS AND
DANCES

BY LEADING LOCAL
TALENT

●

FUN FOR THE
ENTIRE FAMILY

ANNUAL
JAYCEE SPRING MINSTREL

Monroe High School Auditorium
MARCH 11th - 12th
Tickets Now on Sale

SPONSORED BY MONROE JUNIOR CHAMBER OF
COMMERCE

Figure 39: Close-up of same ad.

At that time, Blacks were still suppressed in
Monroe, NC, and elsewhere, and progress for
African Americans was slow to non-existent.

My Brush with Jim Crow

It was an annual tradition for us (Ma, Daddy, and my brothers and sister) to go to our family reunion in Wingate, NC. Ma said, "Poppa always told us children that we needed to come back home the fourth weekend in August. So, when we could, we did."

In the 1950s, during a back-home visit to my grandparents' farm, I got sick. I was sweating more than usual because I had a fever, and occasionally I would vomit.

Ma took me to Monroe to a doctor's office. When we entered the doctor's office, I noticed that there were two waiting rooms. One waiting room was very clean. There was a window, a fan, and green plants next to the chairs in the room.

The second waiting room had benches. There was no window, fan, or plants in this room. This second waiting room was smelly, and so dimly lit that it was downright dark.

The room with the plants and a window was airy and had White people in it. The dark waiting room that had benches and no fan or window contained "Colored people" (as Black people were called then) in it.

As Ma went to sign me in at the desk, she told me to go sit down. I felt miserable, so I looked around and decided to go to the nice waiting room where the plants were. Little did I know that I was crossing a line.

The White people in the nice waiting room looked at me first with surprise and then with anger. The Colored people in the dim and dark waiting room looked out at me in the same way. I had stepped out of my place.

I noticed that many of the people in both rooms were staring at me and beginning to whisper and talk real low to each other.

Both groups felt that, as a Colored person, I was out of place. But what did I know? I felt miserable and was just taking a seat.

During Reconstruction, the US Constitution was changed to say that African Americans should be treated equally. (bbc.co.uk)

But Southern states tried to keep White and Black people separate.

The Supreme Court declared the Black Codes (Jim Crow Laws) legal as long as the laws provided separate but equal facilities.

These laws severely restricted the rights and freedoms of Black Americans. This created a segregated system with separate facilities, such as toilets and waiting rooms, for White and Black people. (bbc.co.uk)

At home up north, I never knew of such distinctions in a doctor's office between waiting rooms for Black folks and White folks in a doctor's office. Everyone just came in and found a seat, and the waiting room looked the same for everybody.

Soon Ma returned and found me. She was a little surprised to see me sitting in the White waiting room; but she said nothing.

About an hour or so later, the Black people's waiting room was empty. The waiting room that I was sitting in, where all the Whites had been waiting had been empty long before. Me and Ma were the last ones in the office.

We waited.

About 10 minutes later, a White nurse came over to where we were sitting and said, "The office is closed. You have to go!"

"WHAT!!" I yelled, as miserable as I felt.

"You heard me," she said. "The office is closed, so leave!"

I looked at Ma. She shook her head and said to me, "Cmon, let's go." I was totally confused.

We got up and left that doctor's office.

Ma was furious! I felt crushed. Why did the nurse talk to us like that? I really felt small, but Ma shocked me when she said, "I forgot where I was. I thought things were better down here than when I was growing up. These White people are still mean and wicked. We will get you well on our own. Do you hear me? DO YOU HEAR ME?" she yelled.

Teary-eyed, I said, "Yes, Ma." I used my left arm to wipe the tears from my eyes and snot from my nose.

Ma never told me directly what that was all about. But I did hear her talking to her sisters, telling them what happened at the doctor's office. One of my aunts said to her, "Ain't nothing changed. These crackers are still evil, and you lucky they didn't call the law on you like they used to do in the past. That's why we all left in the first place. They're still wicked."

A few days later, after some herbs and tea, I felt better. But I will always remember how we got put out of that doctor's office in Monroe and how that White nurse talked to me and Ma like we were nothing.

I realized much later that the separate-but-equal law to me was truly a joke.

I never realized that the Jim Crow laws had a direct impact on me and my family in those days. I was too young to understand any of it, and my parents and grandparents sort of shielded us (the young'uns) from what was happening. They would always tell us, "Go outside," when they were talking big-people talk. We were to be seen but NEVER to be heard. We were forbidden to know any of the legal details of family matters and very little of the ins and outs of the land.

As I think about it now, maybe most of them were farmhands and had very little education. Fifty years prior to the 1900s, Black people were still enslaved and forbidden to read.

By the 1960s, Dr Martin Luthor King's aide reported on the slow-moving progress in North Carolina: "Monroe is still far behind in making the blessings of freedom a reality to all of its citizens." (See complete story in the attached figure.)

The Monroe

YEAR—NO. 69   MONROE, N. C. 28110

1966 9-20-

E-J

...ays Monroe Lags Behind

Racial Progress Slow, Dr. King's Aide Reports

Enquirer Journal

A representative of the Department of Economic Affairs, Southern Christian Leadership Conference, was in Monroe this week for discussions on the Negro's economic status in Monroe.

Reporting on his findings, Rev. Leonard R. Mitchell yesterday made the statement quoted below:

"Upon making inquiries with various Negro civic leaders in the City of Monroe, I have found that the bulk of the statements about racial progress has been exaggerated out of proportion.

"Monroe is still far behind the nation in making the blessings of freedom a reality to all of its citizens. For instance no Negro women are employed at two major industries, although 50 per cent of all Negro women in the city are available for work and several dozen have applied for jobs. Even though these places are singled out, by no means are these the only ones guilty of discrimination.

"Negros are still being harrassed by the police and county deputies without justification. The federal programs that are under the War on Poverty have not been explained in detail to the Negro citizens and have not yet been implemented in the city by the people that would tend

to benefit the most from them.

"Although most places have been desegregated in terms of compliance with the public accommodations Section (Title II) of the Civil Rights Act of 1964, Monroe Negro Americans still suffer from lack of compliance with the Fair Employment (Title VII) Section of the same act.

"As a representative of the Southern Christian Leadership Conference (SCLC) headed by Dr. Martin Luther King, Jr., I personally call upon the business community of Monroe to comply with these provisions without delay.

"In a personal conversation held with Mayor Fred D. Wilson of Monroe, I called upon him to use all power at his disposal to see that federal law is obeyed in Monroe.

"I asked the mayor to see to it that every department of the city government acts without delay to insure the right of every citizen, without regards to race, religion or national orgin, to participate in government, and to receive all funds that are due, that is: welfare, unemployment, Social Security, Etc; and that every effort be made to secure full employment for the citizens of Monroe without delay.

"I called upon the mayor to make jobs available for all its residents thru industry, com-

merce and public works programs of the City of Monroe.

"After talking about police harrassment, Mayor Wilson assured me that he would use his influence to eliminate any harrassment or alleged harrasments that is directed toward any of Monroe's citizens or visitors.

"I strongly recommended to the mayor that he establish a Bi-Racial Commission, composed of people chosen by the groups that they represent, and not by the mayor, to study ways of attracting new industries to the community. These new industries will give Monroe an additional source of tax revenue and help fill the void in jobs. I called upon him, however, to take means to insure that the new industries would be equal employment opportunity employers.

"I further called upon the mayor to instruct the Board of City Planners to continue investigation of the public housing to be built with monies provided by the federal government, and that these houses be open to all citizens qualifying on basis of income without regards to race or any other determining factor. The mayor assured me that construction of these houses will be handled by Equal Employment Opportunity Employers."

Figure 40: Report contributed and highlighted by Gypsy Culp Houston, Genealogy & Local History Librarian, Union County Library, Monroe, North Carolina.

104

In the 1960s, to challenge some of the still-remaining Jim Crow laws, companies began to embrace Affirmative Action and, later on, DEI (Diversity, Equity, and Inclusion).

Affirmative Action

President John F. Kennedy created a Committee on Equal Employment Opportunity in 1961. He issued Executive Order 10925, which used the term "affirmative action" to refer to measures designed to achieve non-discrimination. (U.S. Department of Labor (https://www.dol.gov › agencies › of ccp › faqs › AAFAQsForbeshttps://www.forbes.com › brianbushard › 2024/05/23)

As societal laws began to distance themselves from Affirmative Action, Diversity Equity, and Inclusion emerged on the horizon.

DEI

The birth of DEI also occurred in the 1960s during the civil-rights movement, DEI expanded, becoming more inclusive of different groups (Cooleaf https://www.cooleaf.com › blog › a-history-of-corporate…)

Primary Difference between Diversity and Affirmative Action

Affirmative action is numbers oriented, aimed at changing the demographics within an organization. Managing diversity is behavioral, aimed at changing the organizational culture and developing skills and policies that get the best from everyone. (See About Affirmative Action, Diversity and Inclusion – AAAED and American Association for Acces Equity and Diversity – A.)

On June 29, 2023, the Supreme Court set the United States back decades, invalidating the policy of affirmative action that enabled institutes of higher learning to pursue diversity and equity through admissions.

Florida, Texas, and Utah are among the handful of states whose legislatures have approved bans on DEI efforts in higher education and public offices. In Florida, the Board of Education recently announced a new rule banning public colleges from using state and federal funds on DEI initiatives. This ruling includes the dismissal of African American AP Classes in high school and the banning of Black historical information in school and public libraries.

Joyce Green

Often, those attempting to undo DEI initiatives argue that students—especially White students—are harmed by learning about the history of racism in the United States because it may leave them feeling guilty or ashamed of their identity. (Jun 14, 2024)

"Jim Crow" is alive and well today—just in a different guise.

A Grandma's Thoughts

I often think of the days when I was growing up and the various experiences I went through. My great grandparents and grandparents struggled to maintain their lives and survive enslavement.

Growing Up

Most captured Africans came to the New World in chains. They were enslaved, freed, became share croppers, dealt with Jim Crow, migrated North, and, by the 1960s, participated in integration.

Though the Black Power Movement and integration in the '60s seemed to move Negroes forward, it separated many of us from the cohesiveness and connections we had in our own communities. We directed our desires toward the goal of sounding and looking like Whites in order to be accepted into their world (which we never were).

I was often told to put a clothespin on my nose so that my nose wouldn't be so flat. We were taught to straighten our hair and, when we could afford it, to wear our clothes and our hair like White people. Integration broke down the boundaries we had in our neighborhoods, but I think that we had to go through it to satisfy our desire of what it would be like to be like the Whites or to have made it.

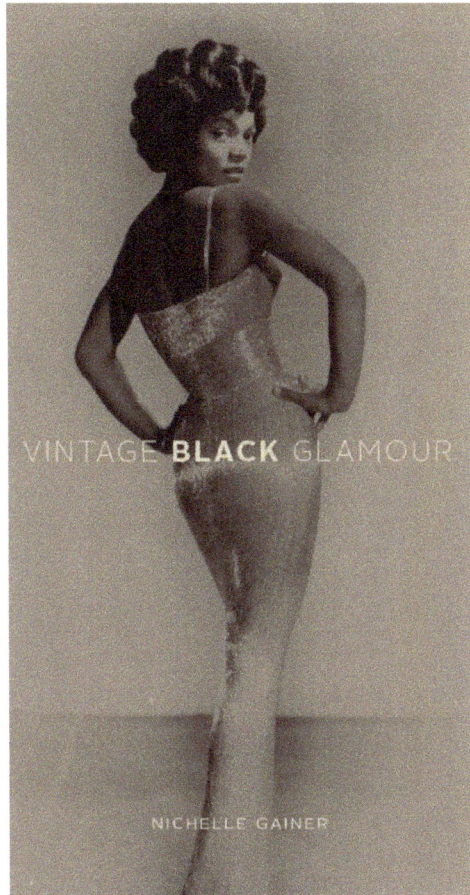

Figure 41: Embracing Black glamour rather than imitating Whites. Dorothea Towels 1950

After more than 400 years of continuous oppression of Blacks, it amazes me that the White so-called civilized descendants of this society who captured, enslaved, and stripped a people of their religion, names, language, identity, and culture, and have a 400-year head start in the progression of life pretend to have amnesia about what their ancestors did and what they continue to do currently. Oftentimes, they blame the system, but who created the system? They continue to totally ignore their 400-plus years of head start and past ruthless behavior while claiming ultimate civility. If they're so civil, why do they fight so hard to ban and suppress the history and achievements of Americans of African descent and then claim to be superior?

It took a while, but why would we Black folks, who relate to a spiritual core, want to follow that path?

I realized that many of my family elders never showed each other or us children any affection. My aunts and uncles were never hugged by grandma or grandpa, and they never hugged each other. That behavior was passed down to me and my brothers and sisters, too.

When I visited my friends, I never saw any affection shown to them, either.

Why did we have this behavior?

One of the laws of the Jim Crow era that affected Black people was the banning of affection and love by Black folks in public.

Black people were not allowed to show public affection toward one another in public, especially kissing, because it offended White people. (Wikipedia)

But it's a new day! BLACK LOVE IS THE KEY!

Why Is Black Love Important?

Black Love has been an act of resistance and a testament to the resiliency of Black people. It has been used to support and build communities. It has allowed Black people to share their woes and dreams and express themselves outside the bounds of whiteness.

But one of the most important things Black love has done is to provide an avenue for us Black Americans to recognize our humanity and acknowledge that we are deserving of love and capable of loving. And, for these reasons, Black love has been revolutionary. ("In Pursuit of Black Love: A Conversation about Black Love & Its Revolutionary Power," by Madison Lyman, *The Kansas City Defender*, February 19, 2024)

MUCH LOVE, FAMILY!

GRANDMA!

www.ingramcontent.com/pod-product-compliance
Lightning Source LLC
Chambersburg PA
CBHW041921090426
42741CB00019B/3442